ii

Governor Arne and First Lady Susan Carlson

Minnesota Times & Tastes

Recipes & Menus
Seasoned with History
from the
**Minnesota Governor's
Residence**

edited by
Jean Steiner

The 1006 Summit Avenue Society is a non-profit organization established in 1982 to help support the Minnesota Governor's Residence. Membership in the society is open to the public.

For information on where to get copies of *Minnesota Times & Tastes*, call the Governor's Residence at (612) 297-2161, or write to:

Minnesota Times & Tastes,
The Governor's Residence,
1006 Summit Avenue,
St. Paul, Minnesota 55105

Library of Congress Number: 93-086792
ISBN Number: 0-9606852-1-9
Manufacturer's Number: 781474

Copyright © 1993
The 1006 Summit Avenue Society
St. Paul, Minnesota 55105
First Edition, All Rights Reserved.

Printed in the United States of America on recycled paper by Gopher State Litho, 3232 East 40th Street, Minneapolis, MN 55406.

Design and desktop publishing by Barbara Ladd, St. Paul, Minnesota

Price $24.95 plus tax
All proceeds from sale of the book go toward maintenance and refurbishing of the Minnesota Governor's Residence

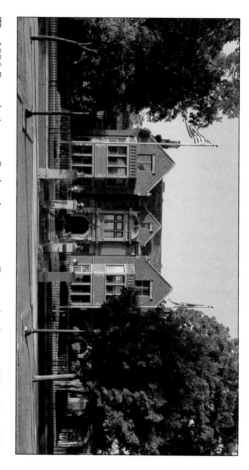

My heartfelt thanks to The 1006 Summit Avenue Society for sponsoring this cookbook project as a fundraiser for the residence; to the many who gave their time and talents and made the project a success; to all the people for whom Minnesota is home, who live near the lakes and wooded areas, in the green valleys and farmlands, in the cities and small towns of this beautiful state; and especially to the children on whom its future depends.

— *Susan Carlson*

v

Contents

Preface

This book salutes Olivia Irvine Dodge, who was born at 1006 Summit Avenue and spent her childhood there, and, who with her sister, gave the house to the State of Minnesota as a Governor's Residence, and who continues her support of the residence.

It honors, too, the first ladies of Minnesota who contributed to the stewardship of the house, who lived there and made it function as a home and an official state house during major renovation and constant, on-going restoration.

They applied their talents and gave generously of their efforts to preserve and enhance the history the house embodies. They are the unsung heroines in the success of the house as a state ceremonial building.

The book is one of First Lady Susan Carlson's fundraising projects for the residence, in cooperation with the 1006 Summit Avenue Society. She wanted a "Minnesota book," and so the most recognizable Minnesota symbol, the loon, appears on its pages.

The bird's clear call is a sound of home in the land of 10,000 lakes, where it summons Minnesotans and visitors to the tranquility of blue skies and waters, farmlands, and wooded countryside that make Minnesota "L'Etoile du Nord" (The Star of the North).

The Carlsons welcome guests to the fundraising 80th birthday celebration for the residence in 1991.

Hospitality
at the
Governor's Residence

"It takes
a heap o' livin'
t' make a house a home."

Edgar Albert Guest

Through the years, the grand old house at 1006 Summit Avenue has welcomed seven families, adapted to their lifestyles, and changed with the times. In the early 1900s, the Horace Irvines, who built the house, filled it with gracious living — servants to help with the children, late-evening garden parties, and holiday celebrations rich in family tradition.

For 52 years, the house served as the Irvine family home. It took on the dual role as a home and state ceremonial house in 1964, when the Irvine chapter of its story closed, and the family gave it to the state for a governor's residence. The state officially accepted the gift in 1965.

The foyer

It's a house where public and private lives merge...

In January 1991, Governor Arne Carlson, First Lady Susan Carlson, and their daughters Anne and Jessica, became the sixth governor's family to move into the country-manor-style house. They brought along Jenny, the family schnauzer and Bandit, their cat. A year and a half later, they adopted Jessica's pet, Daisy, a West Highland Terrier. Their son Tucker, who now makes his home in St. Paul, was living in Rhode Island at the time.

Giant step for a small girl

The move to the residence was a big change for then seven-year-old Jessica. Home for her had been a comfortable, Cape Cod style house, much like all the others in the neighborhood around Lake Owasso in Shoreview, just north of St. Paul, and not at all like the imposing structures she saw as the family drove along wide, tree-lined Summit Avenue.

"That first day here, Jessica seemed so small as she wandered through the high-ceilinged rooms on the first floor, with her hands behind her back and Jenny at her heels, exploring the place," says First Lady Susan.

"She walked from the entrance to the dining room, into the drawing room, down the few steps into the solarium, and back again into the entry way. There she stopped for the second time to look at two large, framed photos on the wall, and she asked us, 'Whose pictures are these?'

"Arne and I explained that they were photos of Mr. and Mrs. Horace Irvine, the first people to live here. She seemed

Guests fill the foyer with warmth and cheer.

Dining room

Library

...where personal mementos become pieces of history...

to accept that answer, but then glanced at them again, and with a puzzled look, said, 'Why didn't they take their pictures with them when they moved?'"

Fast paced beginning

So the Carlsons' time began in the house where public and private lives merge; where personal mementos become pieces of history; where Jessica would outgrow Cabbage Patch dolls and learn to ride her two-wheel bike; where their daughter Anne would have her wedding reception; where almost immediately their home would open to visitors from all over the state and the nation.

"We had little time to settle in," says Susan, "because we had to be ready for meetings and guests that have to do with the job of being governor — legislators and other government dignitaries."

Also, Minnesota was the sports capital of the country then. And at Governor Carlson's invitation, the premier sporting events of '91 and '92 — the Super Bowl, the World Series, the Special Olympics, the Davis Cup, and the Final Four — brought governors and their wives from North Carolina, Ohio, Georgia, Missouri, and Indiana for overnight stays.

In May of '91, Hillary Rodham Clinton, visiting the

Twin Cities for a series of speeches, shared leftover chicken with the Carlsons in the kitchen and spent the night in a guest room. Later she sent a note to tell them that her stay was one of the best times she'd had, "just visiting together and sharing food . . . ." Arnold Schwarzenegger, Jessica's favorite guest, came for lunch while he was in Minnesota promoting the President's Council on Physical Fitness.

A dessert buffet in the dining room draws the attention of Jessica and the first lady.

Drawing room

Solarium

... where ordinary occurrences become special events

In addition, many children have been guests of the Carlsons. Some have come as part of a "read more" challenge the governor and first lady give students when they travel to schools around the state. Those who do additional reading get an invitation to lunch at the Governor's Residence.

"When children come, whether for occasions such as the Schwarzenegger visit, or for Easter egg hunts, Halloween and birthday parties, they always want their usual kind of food," says Susan.

But it seems special to them at the residence, she says, because the house lends a touch of elegance to even chocolate chip cookies, pizza, and hamburgers.

That elegance of yesteryear lingers, too, in the special recipes the residence chefs serve when guests come to dine. The chefs share those selected recipes on pages that follow as First Lady Susan and Governor Carlson invite you in for a glimpse of

life at the residence in the '90s. With photos, bits of history, and recipes from decades past, they welcome you to stay for a look back at the times and tastes of the other families who have lived in the grand old house and made it a home to remember. ◆

Pine boughs and trees, weighted with Minnesota's snow, twinkle with fairy lights at Christmas.

The Carlson family (front row, l. to r.) Anne Carlson Davis, Jessica, First Lady Susan. Back row: Andrew Davis, Tucker Carlson, Governor Arne Carlson. Pets (l. to r.) Daisy and Jenny.